Dennis® and GNASHER JOKES

MARKS & SPENCER

Marks and Spencer p.l.c.
PO Box 3339
Chester CH99 9QS

shop online
www.marksandspencer.com

ISBN-978-1-84960-173-3

Printed in China

Contents

400+ **JOKES**

Family
JOKES

FAMILY JOKES

WHY DID GRANNY PUT WHEELS ON HER ROCKING CHAIR?
She liked to rock and roll!

DENNIS: MUM, WHY DO I HAVE TO GO TO BED?
Mum: Because the bed won't come to you!

DENNIS: GRAN, WHY DO YOU KEEP GOING TO LOOK AT THE LETTER BOX?
Gran: Because my computer keeps telling me I've got mail!

**MUM: DENNIS,
YOU'VE BEEN IN A FIGHT
– YOU'VE LOST YOUR FRONT TEETH!**
*Dennis: No I haven't Mum, they're
in my pocket!*

**DENNIS: GRAN, WHY HAVE YOU
GOT CUSTARD IN ONE EAR AND
JELLY IN THE OTHER?**
*Gran: You'll have to speak up,
dear. I'm a trifle deaf!*

**DENNIS: HELLO DOCTOR, MY
SISTER THINKS SHE'S INVISIBLE!**
Doctor: What sister?

**WHY DID YOUR SISTER
SPEND TWO DAYS STUCK
IN A REVOLVING DOOR?**
*Because she was looking for
the door knob!*

Dennis: Dad, did you hear about the fool who keeps going around saying "No"?
DAD: NO.
Dennis: Oh, so it's you!

Pie-Face: This morning my dad gave me soap flakes instead of corn flakes for breakfast.
CURLY: I BET YOU WERE MAD.
Pie-Face: Mad? I was foaming at the mouth!

**WHAT DO YOU CALL
THE BEST DAD IN THE WORLD?**
Top of the pops!

**DID YOU HEAR ABOUT THE BOY
WHO SLEPT WITH HIS HEAD UNDER
THE PILLOW?**
*When he woke up the tooth
fairies had taken all his teeth!*

**DID YOU HEAR WHAT DAD DID
LAST NIGHT WHEN HE HEARD A
MOUSE SQUEAKING?**
He got up to oil it!

**DID YOU HEAR ABOUT THE
PARENTS WHO CALLED
THEIR BABY 'CAFFEINE'?**
*It kept them up
all night!*

WHY DO THE FRENCH NEVER HAVE TWO EGGS FOR BREAKFAST?
Because one egg is un oeuf!

Dad, I dreamt I was eating a giant marshmallow last night
MUM: THAT'S NICE DEAR
Dad, I woke up coughing feathers and my pillow was missing!

Sports
JOKES

WHAT DO A FOOTBALLER AND A MAGICIAN HAVE IN COMMON?
Both do hat-tricks!

WHICH GOALKEEPER CAN JUMP HIGHER THAN A CROSSBAR?
All of them. A crossbar can't jump!

WHY ARE FOOTBALL PLAYERS NEVER ASKED FOR DINNER?
Because they're always dribbling!

WHY DID THE FOOTBALLER HOLD HIS BOOT TO HIS EAR?
Because he liked sole music!

WHAT PART OF A FOOTBALL PITCH SMELLS NICEST?
The scenter spot!

WHY AREN'T FOOTBALL STADIUMS BUILT IN OUTER SPACE?
Because there is no atmosphere!

WHAT'S THE CHILLIEST GROUND IN THE PREMIERSHIP?
Cold Trafford!

HOW DID THE FOOTBALL PITCH END UP AS A TRIANGLE?
Somebody took a corner!

WHAT DID THE BUMBLEBEE STRIKER SAY?
"Hive scored!"

WHY DID A FOOTBALLER TAKE A PIECE OF ROPE ONTO THE PITCH?
He was the skipper!

WHAT WAS THE GOALKEEPER'S FAVOURITE SNACK?
Beans on post!

HOW DO HENS ENCOURAGE THEIR FOOTBALL TEAMS?
They egg them on!

WHY DIDN'T THE DOG WANT TO PLAY GOLF?
It was a boxer!

WHEN FISH PLAY FOOTBALL, WHO IS THE CAPTAIN?
The team's kipper!

WHERE DO FOOTBALL DIRECTORS GO WHEN THEY ARE FED UP?
The bored room!

WHAT DID THE FOOTBALLER SAY WHEN HE ACCIDENTALLY BURPED DURING A GAME?
Sorry, it was a freak hic!

WHAT SHOULD A FOOTBALL TEAM DO IF THE PITCH IS FLOODED?
Bring on their subs!

WHERE DO OLD BOWLING BALLS END UP?
In the gutter!

SPORTS JOKES

WHAT IS A RUNNER'S FAVOURITE SUBJECT IN SCHOOL?
Jog-raphy!

WHO WON THE RACE BETWEEN TWO BALLS OF STRING?
They we're tied!

WHY WAS THE HOCKEY FIELD SO WET?
The players dribbled all over it!

WHICH TWO FOOTBALL TEAMS ALWAYS START WITH A 3,5,2 FORMATION?
Table football teams!

WHAT HAS 22 LEGS, 11 HEADS AND 2 WINGS?
A football team!

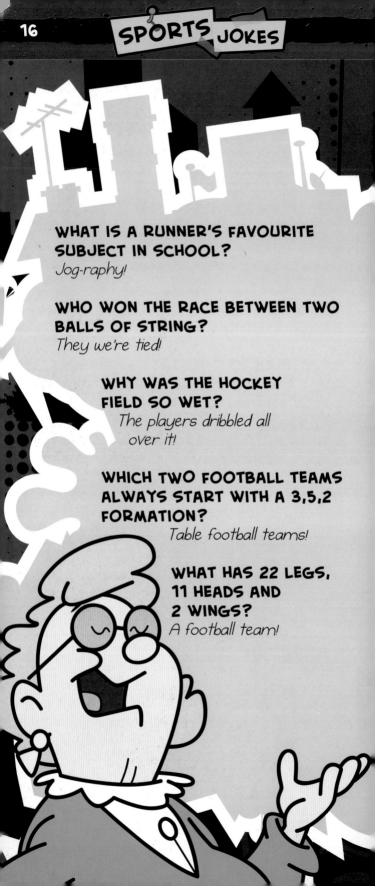

Animal
JOKES

DAD: HAVE YOU PUT THE CAT OUT?
Dennis: Why, is it on fire?

WHAT DO YOU CALL A TERRIFIED DINOSAUR?
A nervous rex!

HOW DO YOU TAKE A LION'S TEMPERATURE?
Very carefully!

WHAT DO DINOSAURS USE TO CUT DOWN TREES?
Dinosaws!

WHERE DID THE STUPID WOODWORM LIVE?
In a brick!

WHAT DO YOU DO WHEN TWO SNAILS HAVE A FIGHT?
Leave them to slug it out!

WHAT DO YOU GET IF YOU CROSS AN ELEPHANT WITH A KANGAROO?
Big holes all across Australia!

WHAT HAS ANTLERS AND SUCKS BLOOD?
A moose-quito!

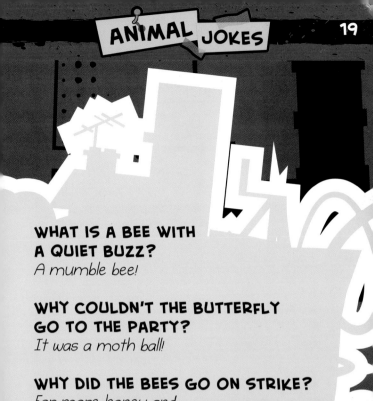

**WHAT IS A BEE WITH
A QUIET BUZZ?**
A mumble bee!

**WHY COULDN'T THE BUTTERFLY
GO TO THE PARTY?**
It was a moth ball!

WHY DID THE BEES GO ON STRIKE?
*For more honey and
shorter flowers!*

**WHAT DO YOU CALL A FUNNY
HORSE RACER?**
A jokey!

**WHAT DO YOU GET IF YOU CROSS
A CAT WITH A PARROT?**
A carrot!

**WHAT DID THE SARDINE CALL
THE SUBMARINE?**
A can of people!

**WHAT IS A FRENCH CAT'S
FAVOURITE PUDDING?**
Chocolate mouse!

WHAT DO YOU GET IF CROSS A CAT WITH A CANARY?
Shredded tweet!

WHAT DO YOU CALL A CAT WITH EIGHT LEGS THAT LIKES TO SWIM?
An octopuss!

HOW DO YOU KNOW THAT CATS ARE SENSITIVE CREATURES?
They never cry over spilt milk!

WHAT DO YOU GET IF YOU CROSS A CAT WITH FATHER CHRISTMAS?
Santa Claws!

WHAT DO CATS READ IN THE MORNING?
Mewspapers!

WHAT DOES A CAT CALL A BOWL OF MICE?
A purrfect meal!

WHAT KIND OF DOG DOES A VAMPIRE PREFER?
A bloodhound!

WHY DID THE POOR DOG CHASE HIS OWN TAIL?
He was trying to make both ends meet!

HOW CAN YOU TELL IF YOU HAVE A STUPID DOG?
It chases parked cars!

WHAT HAPPENS WHEN IT RAINS CATS AND DOGS?
You can step in a poodle!

WHAT DID THE HUNGRY DALMATIAN SAY WHEN HE HAD A MEAL?
That hit the spots!

WHY DON'T DOGS MAKE GOOD DANCERS?
Because they have two left feet!

HOW DO YOU STOP A DOG SMELLING?
Put a peg on its nose!

WHAT DO YOU GET IF YOU CROSS A GUN DOG WITH A TELEPHONE?
A golden receiver!

WHAT HAPPENS TO A DOG THAT KEEPS EATING BITS OFF THE TABLE?
He gets splinters in his mouth!

WHAT IS THE ONLY KIND OF DOG YOU CAN EAT?
A hot dog!

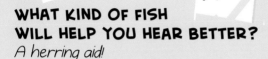

**WHAT KIND OF FISH
WILL HELP YOU HEAR BETTER?**
A herring aid!

WHERE DO FISH WASH?
In a river basin!

**WHAT'S THE LAST THING THAT GOES
THROUGH A FLY'S MIND WHEN IT HITS
A WINDSCREEN?**
Its bottom!

**HOW DO YOU KNOW WHICH END
OF A WORM IS ITS HEAD?**
Wait for it to burp!

**WHAT DO YOU GIVE A BUTTERFLY
WITH A SORE THROAT?**
Antiseptic moth wash!

WHAT DO YOU GIVE AN ANT WITH A SORE THROAT?
Ant-iseptic!

WHAT IS GREY, HAS BIG EARS AND A TRUNK?
A mouse on holiday!

WHAT DO YOU CALL AN ARCTIC COW?
An eskimoo!

WHO GRANTS FISH THREE WISHES?
The Fairy Codmother!

WHAT FISH CAN FIX PIANOS?
A tuna fish!

WHY DO BIRDS FLY SOUTH IN THE WINTER?
Because they can't afford the bus fare!

WHAT IS BLACK AND WHITE AND BLACK AND WHITE AND BLACK AND WHITE?
A penguin rolling down a hill!

WHAT HAS FOUR LEGS AND GOES OOM OOM?
A cow walking backwards!

WHAT HAS FOUR LEGS AND GOES OOW OOW?
A cow in Australia!

WHAT'S THE DIFFERENCE BETWEEN A CAT AND A FROG?
A cat has nine lives but a frog croaks every night!

HOW DO FISH TIE THEIR SHOELACES?
They don't have shoelaces, they only have soles!

WHAT DO GIRAFFES HAVE THAT OTHER ANIMALS DON'T HAVE?
Baby giraffes!

WHY DON'T GRASSHOPPERS PLAY FOOTBALL?
They prefer cricket!

WHAT GOES 99-THUMP, 99-THUMP, 99-THUMP?
A centipede with a wooden leg!

WHAT'S GREEN AND HANGS FROM TREES?
Monkey snot!

WHAT'S GREEN AND HANGS FROM CAVES?
A sick bat!

WHAT'S THE SLOWEST ANIMAL ON EARTH?
A snail with a limp!

WHAT'S THE FASTEST ANIMAL ON EARTH?
A snail with a rocket strapped to its back!

WHY SHOULDN'T YOU TAKE A CROCODILE TO THE ZOO?
Because they'd rather go to the cinema!

WHY DID THE CHICKEN CROSS THE ROAD IN THE FIRST PLACE?
No one is eggs-actly sure!

WHY DID THE SECOND CHICKEN CROSS THE ROAD?
He did it as a yolk!

WHAT'S THE BEST WAY OF COUNTING COWS?
With a cow-culator!

WHAT DO YOU CALL A SHEEP WITH A PARACHUTE?
A woolly jumper!

WHAT DO YOU CALL A SHEEP WITH A PARACHUTE THAT PUSHES IN FRONT OF YOU?
A woolly queue jumper!

WHY DO SHARKS LIVE IN SALTWATER?

Because pepper makes them sneeze!

WHAT IS A CAT'S FAVOURITE BREAKFAST CEREAL?

Mice crispies!

WHAT'S A MOUSE'S FAVOURITE BREAKFAST CEREAL?

Bubble and squeak!

ARE DOLPHINS EVER NAUGHTY BY ACCIDENT?

No, they always do it on porpoise!

WHY DO DUCKS HAVE WEBBED FEET?

So they can kick spiders!

WHAT ARE INVISIBLE AND SMELL OF CARROTS?

Rabbit farts!

WHY DO HUMMINGBIRDS HUM?

Because they don't know the words!

HOW DO YOU STOP BIRDS BUILDING NESTS?
Take away their tool belts!

WHERE DO DINOSAURS WEAR TIES?
Around their tyrannosaurus necks!

WHAT DO YOU GET IF YOU CROSS A CROCODILE WITH A FLOWER?
I don't know, but I'm not getting close enough to smell it!

HOW DID NOAH SEE THE ANIMALS IN THE ARK AT NIGHT?
By flood lighting!

WHAT DO YOU CALL AN ELEPHANT THAT HAS HAD TOO MUCH TO DRINK?
Trunk!

WHAT DO YOU CALL A KANGAROO AT THE NORTH POLE?
Lost!

WHAT DO YOU CALL A RABBIT DRESSED UP AS A CAKE?
A cream bun!

WHAT DO YOU CALL A DOG THAT IS ALWAYS GETTING INTO FIGHTS?
A boxer!

WHAT DO YOU CALL A COW THAT CUTS GRASS?
A lawn mooooer!

IN WHAT HIGH-FLYING TOWN DO PARROTS MAKE FILMS?
Pollywood!

WHAT DO YOU CALL A CHICKEN THAT EATS CEMENT?
A bricklayer!

WHAT DO YOU CALL A FLEA THAT LIVES IN AN IDIOT'S EAR?
A space invader!

WHAT DO YOU GET IF YOU CROSS A RABBIT AND A FLEA?
Bugs Bunny!

HOW DO YOU START AN INSECT RACE?
One, two, flea, go!

HOW DO YOU FIND WHERE A FLEA HAS BITTEN YOU?
Start from scratch!

WHAT HAPPENED WHEN THE CHEF FOUND A DADDY LONG LEGS IN THE SALAD?
It became a daddy short legs!

WHY DID THE SPIDER BUY A CAR?
So he could take it out for a spin!

WHY SHOULD SPIDERS BE GOOD SWIMMERS?
They have webbed feet!

HOW DO YOU SPOT A MODERN SPIDER?
He doesn't have a web, he has a website!

WHAT DO BEES DO IF THEY WANT TO USE PUBLIC TRANSPORT?
Wait at a buzz stop!

WHAT DOES A QUEEN BEE DO WHEN SHE BURPS?
She issues a royal pardon!

WHO IS THE BEE'S FAVOURITE CLASSICAL COMPOSER?
Bee-thoven!

WHAT'S MORE DANGEROUS THAN BEING WITH A FOOL?
Fooling with a bee!

WHAT DID THE BEE SAY TO THE NAUGHTY BEE?
Bee-hive yourself!

WHY DID THE MOSQUITO GO TO THE DENTIST?
To improve his bite!

WHAT IS THE MOST RELIGIOUS INSECT?
A mosque-ito!

WHY WAS THE GLOW-WORM SO UNHAPPY?
Because her children weren't that bright!

HOW CAN YOU TELL WHICH END OF A WORM IS WHICH?
Tickle it in the middle and see which end laughs!

**HOW DO YOU MAKE A
GLOW-WORM HAPPY?**
Cut off its tail and it'll be de-lighted!

WHY ARE ALL MOSQUITOS RELIGIOUS?
They prey on you!

**WHAT DID THE WOODWORM
SAY TO THE CHAIR?**
It's been nice gnawing you!

**WHO WAS THE FIRST WORM
PRIME MINISTER?**
Maggot Thatcher!

**HOW CAN YOU TELL IF YOU'RE
LOOKING AT A POLICE
GLOW-WORM?**
It has a blue light!

WHEN SHOULD YOU STOP FOR A GLOW-WORM?
When he has a red light!

WHAT KIND OF WIG CAN HEAR?
An earwig!

HOW DO YOU KNOW IF YOUR KITCHEN FLOOR IS DIRTY?
The slugs leave a trail on the floor that reads 'clean me'!

**WHY WAS THE MOTH
SO UNPOPULAR?**
He kept picking holes in everything!

**WHAT PILLAR DOESN'T NEED
HOLDING UP?**
A caterpillar!

WHAT DOES A CAT LIKE TO SLEEP ON?
A caterpillow!

**HOW DO WE KNOW THAT
INSECTS ARE SO CLEVER?**
*Because they always know when
you're eating outside!*

**WHAT DOES A CAT LIKE TO EAT
ON HIS BIRTHDAY?**
Jelly and mice cream!

**WHAT HAPPENED WHEN THE WIZARD
TURNED A NAUGHTY BOY INTO
A HARE?**
*He didn't stop rabbiting
on about it!*

**DID YOU HEAR ABOUT THE
BOY WHO SAT
UNDERNEATH A COW?**
He got a pat on the head!

**WHAT IS AN INSECT'S
FAVOURITE GAME?**
Cricket!

**WHAT HAS FOUR WHEELS
AND FLIES?**
A rubbish bin!

**DID YOU HEAR ABOUT THE
MONKEY WHO LEFT BITS
OF HIS LUNCH ALL OVER
THE COMPUTER?**
His dad went bananas!

WHAT WAS THE SNAIL DOING ON THE MOTORWAY?
About one mile a week!

WHAT DO INSECTS LEARN AT SCHOOL?
Mothmatics!

WHAT INSECT LIVES ON NOTHING?
A moth, because it eats holes!

WHAT'S THE BIGGEST MOTH IN THE WORLD?
A mam-moth!

WHAT'S THE BEST DAY FOR MONKEY BUSINESS?
The first of Ape-ril!

HOW DOES MOBY DICK CELEBRATE HIS BIRTHDAY?
He has a whale of a time!

WHERE DO YOU FIND A BIRTHDAY PRESENT FOR A CAT?
A cat-alogue!

WHY WOULDN'T ANYONE EAT THE DOG'S BIRTHDAY CAKE?
Because he always slobbers out the candles!

HOW DO YOU KNOW IF AN ELEPHANT'S BEEN TO YOUR BIRTHDAY PARTY?
Look for his footprints in the ice cream!

WHAT HAS WINGS, A LONG TAIL AND A WEARS A BOW?
A birthday pheasant!

School
JOKES

MRS. CREECHER: NAME A LIQUID THAT DOESN'T FREEZE.
Dennis: Hot water!

WHERE DO YOU LEARN HOW TO MAKE ICING?
Sundae school!

MRS. CREECHER: DID YOU TAKE A BATH THIS MORNING?
Pie-Face: No Miss, is there one missing?

WHAT DO YOU CALL SOMEONE WHO KEEPS TALKING WHEN NO ONE IS LISTENING?
A teacher!

WHY DID THE BOY EAT HIS HOMEWORK?
His teacher told him it would be a piece of cake!

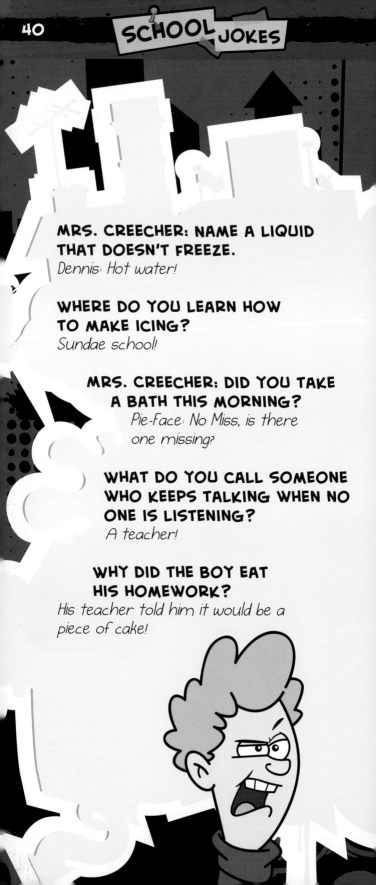

WHAT IS A BIRD'S FAVOURITE SUBJECT?
Owl-gebra!

WHAT INSECT IS GOOD AT MATHS?
An account-ant!

WHY DID THE TEACHER PUT THE LIGHTS ON?
Because the class was so dim!

TEACHER: MAKE UP A SENTENCE USING THE WORD 'LETTUCE'!
Pupil: Lettuce out of school early!

TEACHER: THAT'S QUITE A COUGH YOU HAVE THERE, WHAT ARE YOU TAKING FOR IT?
Pupil: I don't know, teacher! What will you give me?

TEACHER: YOU AREN'T PAYING ATTENTION TO ME. ARE YOU HAVING TROUBLE HEARING?
Pupil: No, teacher! I'm having trouble listening!

TEACHER: YOU MISSED SCHOOL YESTERDAY DIDN'T YOU?
Pupil: Not very much!

FATHER: I HEAR YOU SKIPPED SCHOOL TO PLAY FOOTBALL?
Son: No I didn't, and I have the fish to prove it!

TEACHER: I'D LIKE TO GO THROUGH ONE WHOLE DAY WITHOUT HAVING TO TELL YOU OFF.
Pupil: You have my permission!

BE SURE THAT YOU GO STRAIGHT HOME.
I can't, I live just round the corner!

MAKE A LAUGH AND THE CLASS LAUGHS WITH YOU. BUT YOU GET DETENTION ALONE!

WHAT'S THE WORST THING YOU'LL FIND IN THE SCHOOL CANTEEN?
The food!

WHAT DO FRENCH PUPILS SAY AFTER FINISHING THEIR SCHOOL DINNERS?
Mercy!

**DID YOU HEAR ABOUT
THE CRUEL SCHOOL COOK?**
*She beats the eggs and
whips the cream!*

**PUPIL: THERE IS A DEAD FLY
IN MY DINNER.**
*Cook: Oh dear, I wonder
if it died after tasting it!*

**WHAT'S WORSE THAN FINDING A
CATERPILLAR IN YOUR SALAD?**
Finding half a caterpillar!

**TEACHER: WHY ARE YOU THE
ONLY ONE IN CLASS TODAY?**
*Pupil: Because I missed school
dinner yesterday!*

**PUPIL: I DON'T LIKE CHEESE
WITH HOLES.**
*Dinner Lady: Well just eat
the cheese and leave the
holes on the side
of your plate!*

**TEACHER: THIS IS THE
THIRD TIME I'VE HAD TO TELL YOU OFF
THIS WEEK, WHAT HAVE YOU GOT TO
SAY ABOUT THAT?**
Pupil: Thank heavens it's Friday!

TEACHER: DIDN'T YOU HEAR ME CALL OUT YOUR NAME?
Pupil: Yes, but you said not to answer you back!

DID YOU HEAR ABOUT THE CROSS-EYED TEACHER?
He couldn't control his pupils!

WHY DID THE TEACHER WEAR SUNGLASSES?
Because his class was so bright!

TEACHER: DOES ANYONE KNOW WHICH MONTH HAS 28 DAYS?
Pupil: All of them!

TEACHER: I SAID TO DRAW A COW EATING SOME GRASS BUT YOU'VE ONLY DRAWN THE COW?
Pupil: Yes, the cow ate all the grass!

TEACHER: WHAT'S THE FURTHEST THING YOU CAN SEE FROM THE TOP OF THE EIFFEL TOWER IN PARIS?
Pupil: The Sun!

TEACHER: IN 1940, WHAT WERE THE POLES DOING IN RUSSIA?
Pupil: Holding up the telegraph lines!

TEACHER: WHAT'S YOUR NAME?
Pupil: Fred.
TEACHER: YOU SHOULD SAY "SIR".
Pupil: OK, Sir Fred!

TEACHER: WHAT IS FURTHER AWAY, AUSTRALIA OR THE MOON?
Pupil: Australia, you can see the Moon at night!

TEACHER: WHAT IS THE PLURAL OF MOUSE?
Pupil: Mice.
TEACHER: GOOD, NOW WHAT'S THE PLURAL OF BABY?
Pupil: Twins?

TEACHER: I DESPAIR, FRED, HOW DO YOU MANAGE TO GET SO MANY THINGS WRONG IN A DAY?
Pupil: Because I always get here early sir!

TEACHER: I WISH YOU WOULD PAY A LITTLE ATTENTION.
Pupil: I'm paying as little as I can!

TEACHER: WHAT ARE YOU READING?
Pupil: I don't know.
TEACHER: BUT YOU'RE READING ALOUD!
Pupil: I'm not listening!

WHAT'S THE DIFFERENCE BETWEEN HOMEWORK AND BREAKFAST?
Gnasher didn't eat Dennis's breakfast!

WHY DID CURLY EAT DENNIS'S HOMEWORK?
Because Gnasher wasn't hungry!

WHAT HAS 20 FEET AND SOUNDS AWFUL?
The school choir!

MRS. CREECHER: CLASS, PLEASE BE QUIET TODAY, I HAVE AN AWFUL HEADACHE!
Curly: Why don't you do what my Mum does when she has a headache?
MRS. CREECHER: WHAT'S THAT?
Curly: She sends us out to play!

WHAT HAS A Q AND LOTS OF P'S AND SMELLS AWFUL?
School dinners!

MRS. CREECHER: DENNIS, WHO BROKE THAT WINDOW?
Dennis: It was Walter, he ducked when I threw a ball at him!

EXCUSES FOR NOT DOING YOUR HOMEWORK!

I lost it fighting this kid who said you weren't the best teacher in the school.

Some aliens from outer space borrowed it so they could study how the human brain worked.

I put it in a safe, but lost the combination.

I loaned it to a friend, but he suddenly moved away.

Our furnace stopped working and we had to burn it to stop ourselves from freezing.

I left it in my shirt and my mother put it in the washing machine.

My little sister Bea ate it.

Another pupil fell in a lake and I jumped in to rescue him. Sadly my homework drowned.

I used it to fill a hole in my shoe, you wouldn't want it now.

I didn't do it, because I didn't want the other kids in the class to look bad.

Monster JOKES

WHAT KIND OF BEANS DO ZOMBIES LIKE TO EAT?
Human beans!

HOW DO UNDERTAKERS SPEAK?
Gravely!

WHAT DAY OF THE WEEK DO MONSTERS EAT PEOPLE?
Chews-day!

HOW DO MONSTERS LIKE TO HAVE THEIR EGGS?
Terri-fried!

**WHY IS IT SAFE TO
TELL A MUMMY YOUR SECRET?**
It'll keep it under wraps!

**WHERE DOES A BABY GHOST GO
WHILE ITS PARENTS ARE AT WORK?**
Dayscare!

**HOW DO YOU GET TO THE
MONSTER'S HOUSE?**
*Walk down the street, then
turn fright at the dead end!*

**WHAT DO YOU GET IF YOU CROSS
A RABBIT WITH A WEREWOLF?**
A hare-wolf!

**DO MONSTERS EAT POPCORN
WITH THEIR FINGERS?**
*No, they eat the fingers
seperately!*

**MUMMY: WHERE DO FLEAS
GO IN THE WINTER?**
Werewolf: Search me!

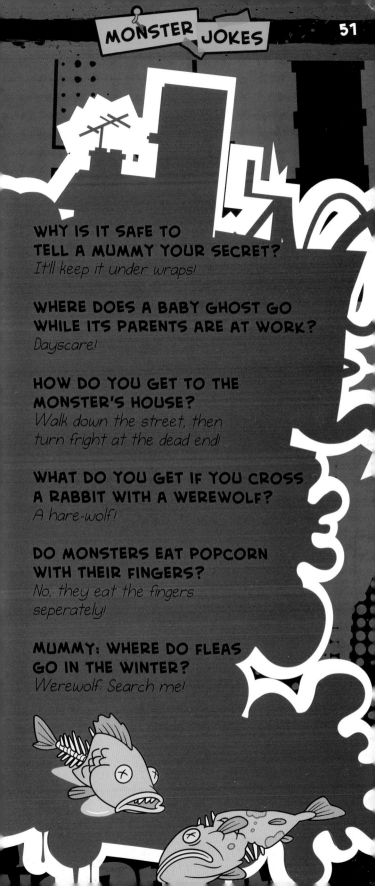

HOW CAN YOU HELP A STARVING CANNIBAL?
Give them a hand!

WHAT SHOULD YOU DO IF YOU GO OUT FOR A PICNIC WITH KING KONG?
Give him the biggest bananas!

WHAT DO CANNIBALS EAT AT PICNICS?
Hard boiled legs!

WHAT HAPPENED AT THE CANNIBAL'S WEDDING?
They toasted the bride and groom!

KNOCK, KNOCK
Who's there?
DONNA
Donna who?
DONNA LOOK NOW BUT THERE'S A BIG MONSTER BEHIND YOU!

WHY DO GHOSTS ALWAYS HANG AROUND IN THREES?
Because two's company and three's a shroud!

WHAT DO YOU CALL A FRIEND WHO IS A SKELETON?
A bony crony!

WHICH MONSTER PLAYS THE MOST PRACTICAL JOKES?
Prankenstein!

WHY DID THE VAMPIRE BECOME AN ARTIST?
Because he was so good at drawing blood!

WHAT IS DRACULA'S FAVOURITE FRUIT?
Neck-tarines!

WHAT IS A GHOST'S FAVOURITE ICE-CREAM FLAVOUR?
Shockolate Chip!

WHY DIDN'T THE SKELETON GO BUNGEE JUMPING?
He didn't have the guts!

WHY DID THE WITCHES WEAR NAME TAGS?
So they know which witch is which!

WHERE DO ZOMBIES HOST PARTIES?
In a rave-yard!

HOW DO MONSTERS COMMUNICATE?
By terror-phone!

WHAT DID THE GHOST SAY TO THE VAMPIRE?
Do you believe in people?

DENNIS: THERE'S A MONSTER AT THE DOOR WITH A REALLY UGLY FACE.
Dad: Tell him you've already got one!

WHERE DO GHOSTS LIKE TO SWIM?
The Dead Sea!

WHY DID THE SMELLY ZOMBIE STAY IN BED?
He felt rotten!

WHAT KIND OF MUSIC DO MUMMIES LISTEN TO?
Wrap music!

WHY DO SOME MONSTERS HAVE LOTS OF EARS?
To make them look more eerie!

WHAT DO YOU CALL GHOST TWINS?
Dead ringers!

DID YOU HEAR ABOUT THE ZOMBIE WHO WENT ON A CRUISE SHIP?
In the restaurant he refused the menu and asked for the passenger list instead!

WHAT'S A MONSTER'S FAVOURITE GAME?
Swallow the leader!

WHAT DO YOU CALL A FAT VAMPIRE?
Count Fatula!

WHAT POSITION DID THE GHOST PLAY IN THE SCHOOL FOOTBALL TEAM?
The ghoul-keeper!

WHAT IS A SKELETON'S FAVOURITE TYPE OF JOKE?
A rib-tickler!

WHAT IS A VAMPIRE'S FAVOURITE BOAT?
A blood vessel!

WHO DID FRANKENSTEIN TAKE TO THE HALLOWEEN PARTY?
His ghoul-friend!

WHAT IS A SEA MONSTER'S FAVOURITE MEAL?
Fish and ships!

WHAT DO YOU GET IF YOU CROSS GODZILLA WITH A DOG?
A scared postman!

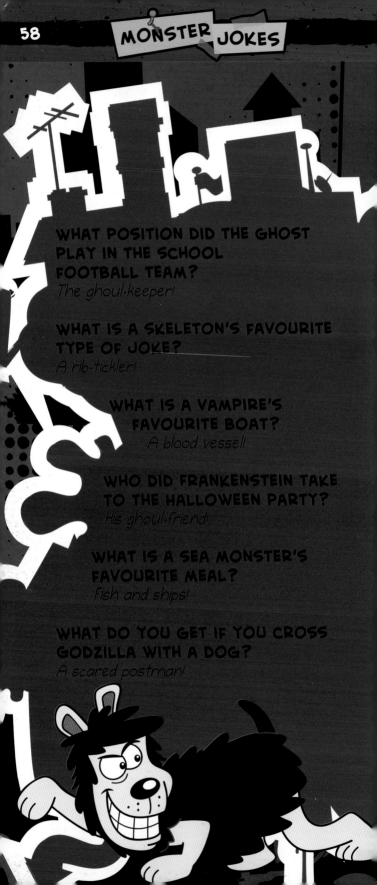

**WHAT DO YOU CALL
A SKELETON WHO WON'T
GET OUT OF BED?**
Lazy bones!

**WHY DID THE WITCH BUY A
NEW COMPUTER?**
Because it had a spell checker!

**WHY WAS THE EGYPTIAN
GIRL WORRIED?**
*Because her Daddy
was a Mummy!*

WHO WAS THE VAMPIRE DESTINED TO FALL IN LOVE WITH?
The girl necks door!

Boy monster: You've got a face like a million dollars.
GIRL MONSTER: HAVE I REALLY?
Boy monster: Yes, it's green and wrinkly!

WHAT DOES THE HUNGRY MONSTER GET AFTER HE'S EATEN TOO MUCH ICE CREAM?
More ice cream!

**WHAT DO YOU GET
IF YOU CROSS A BOY SCOUT
WITH A ZOMBIE?**
*A creature that scares
old ladies across the road!*

**DID YOU HEAR ABOUT THE DOCTOR
WHO CROSSED A PARROT WITH
A VAMPIRE?**
*It bit his neck, sucked his blood
and said 'Who's a pretty boy then?'*

WHAT DID THE WITCH ASK FOR AT THE HOTEL?
Broom Service!

WHY KIND OF COFFEE DO VAMPIRES LIKE TO DRINK?
De-coffinated!

WHAT KIND OF MONSTER LOVES TO DANCE?
A boogie-man!

WHY DID THE VAMPIRE'S LUNCH GIVE HIM HEARTBURN?
It was a stake sandwich!

WHAT DO ZOMBIES TAKE FOR A BAD COLD?
Coffin drops!

Random
JOKES

WHAT'S BIG AND RED AND STANDS IN THE CORNER?
A naughty bus!

WHAT DO YOU CALL A GIRL WITH A TENNIS BALL ON HER HEAD?
An-nette!

WHAT DO YOU CALL A GIRL WITH ONE LEG SHORTER THAN THE OTHER?
Ei-leen!

HOW DOES ROBIN HOOD TIE HIS SHOELACES?
With a bow!

WHAT WERE THE GANGSTER'S LAST WORDS?
Who put that violin in my violin case!

WHAT DO YOU CALL AN AMERICAN DRAWING?
A Yankee doodle!

HOW DO WELSH PEOPLE EAT CHEESE?
Caerphilly!

DENNIS: HAVE YOU EVER SEEN A DUCHESS?
Pie-Face: Yes, it's the same as an English 's'!

WHY DID THE COWBOY DIE WITH HIS BOOTS ON?
Because he didn't want to stub his toe when he kicked the bucket!

HOW DOES A BARBER CUT THE MOON'S HAIR?
Eclipse it!

LAST NIGHT THERE WAS A BIG FIGHT IN THE LOCAL FISH AND CHIP SHOP...
A lot of fish got battered!

POSTMAN: IS THIS LETTER FOR YOU? THE NAME IS SMUDGED.
Pie-Face: No, it can't be for me, my name is Pie-Face!

WHAT IS WHITE AND FURRY AND SMELLS OF MINT?
A polo bear!

DAD WAS DRIVING DOWN THE MOTORWAY WHEN HIS CAR PHONE RANG. IT WAS MUM, URGENTLY WARNING HIM: "I JUST HEARD ON THE NEWS THAT THERE'S A CAR GOING THE WRONG WAY ON THE MOTORWAY. PLEASE BE CAREFUL!"
"It's not just one car!" said Dad
"There are hundreds of them!"

WHY DID THE COLONEL HAVE HIS SUNDIAL FLOODLIT?
So he could tell the time at night.

WHAT DID BATMAN SAY TO ROBIN BEFORE THEY GOT IN THE BATMOBILE?
Get in the car, Robin!

WHY DID THE NEWLYWEDS FEEL SO HOT?
Because people kept toasting them!

WHAT DID THE BIG CANDLE SAY TO THE LITTLE CANDLE?
You're too young to go out!

WALTER: WERE ANY FAMOUS PEOPLE BORN ON YOUR BIRTHDAY?
Dennis: No, just little babies!

WHAT DID THE POLICEMAN SAY TO HIS BELLY BUTTON?
You're under a vest!

WHY WAS THE NOSE SO TIRED?
Because it had been running all day!

WHY DID THE SEAWEED BLUSH?
Because it saw the ship's bottom!

WHAT HAS A BOTTOM AT THE TOP?
Your legs!

**HOW DO YOU KNOW
IF YOU'VE BEEN MADE
UPSIDE DOWN?**
Your nose runs and your feet smell!

**WHY IS SUNDAY STRONGER
THAN MONDAY?**
Because Monday is a weak-day!

**WHAT DO YOU GET IF YOU CROSS
A RIVER AND A STREAM?**
Wet!

WHY WAS THE SAND WET?
Because the sea weed!

WHAT DO YOU GET IF YOU CROSS A UFO WITH A RASHER OF BACON?
A frying saucer!

WHAT DID ONE COMET SAY TO THE OTHER?
Pleased to meteor!

WHAT STARTS WITH 'E', ENDS WITH 'E' AND ONLY HAS ONE LETTER?
An envelope!

HOW DO YOU DOUBLE YOUR MONEY?
Look at it in the mirror!

WHAT SHOULD YOU DO IF YOU SPLIT YOUR SIDES LAUGHING?
Run until you get a stitch!

**WHAT DO YOU CALL
A BOY WHO LIKES ROLLING
IN LEAVES?**
Russell!

**WHAT DO YOU CALL A BOY WHO
LIKES FLOATING IN THE SEA?**
Bob!

WHAT DO YOU GET IF YOU DIAL 666?
The Australian police!

**HOW MANY SOFTIES DOES IT
TAKE TO CHANGE A LIGHT BULB?**
*None. They get their Mumsies
to do it for them!*

HOW MANY GNASHERS DOES IT TAKE TO CHANGE A LIGHTBULB?
None. Who do you think broke it in the first place!

Knock knock!
WHO'S THERE?
Aitch.
AITCH WHO?
I'll come back when your cold is better!

WHAT DO YOU CALL A BOY WITH A PLANK ON HIS HEAD?
Ed-wood!

WHAT DO YOU CALL A BOY WITH A SEAGULL ON HIS HEAD?
Cliff!

**HOW DO SPACEMEN
TIE THEIR SHOELACES?**
With astro-knots!

Knock knock!
WHO'S THERE?
The engineer.
THE ENGINEER WHO?
*The engineer who has come to change
your doorbell!*

DENNIS: I THINK THIS VIOLIN IS BROKEN.
Dad: Well stop eating it then!

HOW MANY RUDE PEOPLE DOES IT TAKE TO CHANGE A LIGHTBULB?
None of your business!

WHAT'S PINK AND WOBBLES?
A jelly baby!

WHAT DO YOU GET IF YOU PUT WALTER'S FAVOURITE TOY IN THE FREEZER?
A teddy-brrrrrr!

WHAT DO YOU GET IF YOU RUN OVER WALTER'S FAVOURITE TOY WITH A LAWNMOWER?
A shreddy-bear!

WHAT DO YOU CALL A GIRL WITH A CHURCH ON HER HEAD?
Abbey!

WHAT DO YOU CALL A GIRL WITH A DRAUGHTY CHURCH ON HER HEAD?
Abi-gale!

WHAT TOOL CAN HELP YOU WITH YOUR MATHS HOMEWORK?
Multi-pliers!

Knock knock!
WHO'S THERE?
Boo.
BOO WHO?
Don't cry, it's only a joke!

WHAT DO YOU CALL AN ESKIMO'S HOUSE WITH NO TOILET?
An ig!

WHAT DO YOU CALL A SNOWMAN IN THE DESERT?
A puddle!

**WHY IS SIX AFRAID
OF SEVEN?**
Because seven eight nine!

**WHY IS SATURDAY NIGHT IMPORTANT
TO JULIUS'S GIRLFRIEND?**
Because thats when Julius Caesar!

WHAT SPACIOUS CAR LIVES IN PARIS?
The hatchback of Notre Dame!

**WHY DID THE MAN LEAVE
RUBBISH ALL OVER HIS TABLE
IN THE RESTAURANT?**
*He thought it was polite to
leave a tip!*

HOW MANY EGGS DOES IT TAKE TO MAKE A STINK BOMB?
Quite a phew!

WHAT GAME IS THE SMELLIEST TO PLAY?
Ping pong!

WHAT WAS WRONG WITH WOODEN CARS?
They wooden go!

WHY DON'T TRAFFIC LIGHTS GO SWIMMING?
Because they take forever to change!

HOW DID THE TELEPHONES GET MARRIED?
In a double ring ceremony!

WHY DID THE CHILD STUDY IN THE AEROPLANE?
He wanted a higher education!

WHY WAS THE BROOM LATE?
It over swept!

IF IRELAND SANK
INTO THE SEA, WHAT COUNTY
WOULDN'T SINK?
Cork!

HOW DO WE KNOW THAT THE EARTH
WON'T COME TO AN END?
Because it's round!

WHY DID THE STUPID RACING
DRIVER MAKE TEN PIT STOPS
DURING THE RACE?
He was asking for directions!

WHY DID THE BURGLAR TAKE
A SHOWER?
He wanted to make a clean getaway!

WHY DID E.T. HAVE SUCH BIG EYES?
Because he saw his phone bill!

WHAT'S WORSE THAN RAINING CATS AND DOGS?
Hailing taxis!

WHAT KIND OF HAIR DO OCEANS HAVE?
Wavy!

WHAT RUNS BUT NEVER WALKS?
Water!

HOW DO YOU MAKE MILK SHAKE?
Give it a good scare!

Dennis: Did you hear about the mad scientist who invented an acid that could burn through anything?
CURLY: NO, WHAT ABOUT HIM?
Dennis: Now he's trying to invent something to hold it in!

Customer: Is this a second hand shop?

SHOPKEEPER: YES SIR.

Customer: Good. Can you fit one to my watch then, please?

CUSTOMER: DO YOU HAVE ANY INVISIBLE INK?

Shopkeeper: Certainly Sir, what colour would you like?

PIE-FACE: THIS MATCH WON'T LIGHT?

Curly: That's funny. It did this morning?

WHY ARE YOU COVERED IN BRUISES?
I started walking through a revolving door and I changed my mind!

WHY IS IT DANGEROUS TO SLEEP ON TRAINS?
Because trains run over sleepers!

WHY DID THE SWORD SWALLOWER SWALLOW AN UMBRELLA?
He wanted to put something away for a rainy day!

WHAT LIES AT THE BOTTOM OF THE SEA AND SHIVERS?
A nervous wreck!

WHAT DO YOU GET IF YOU CROSS A ROAD WITH A SAFARI PARK ?
Double yellow lions!

WHAT DO YOU GET IF YOU CROSS AN ARTIST WITH A POLICEMAN?
A brush with the law!

WHERE DOES THE COLONEL KEEP HIS ARMIES?
Up his sleevies!

WHAT DID THE TIE SAY TO THE HAT?
You go on a-head and I'll hang around!

Dennis: I think my alarm clock is made of cheese.
DAD: WHY?
Dennis: Because it keeps going off!

WHAT DID THE PICTURE SAY TO THE WALL?
I've got you covered!

DID YOU HEAR ABOUT THE CHICKEN THAT PLAYED FOOTBALL?
It was booked for fowl play!

WHY DID THE LAZY MAN WANT A JOB IN A BAKERY?
So he could just loaf around!

DENNIS: DO YOU LOOK IN A MIRROR AFTER YOU WASH YOUR FACE?
Curly: No, I look into a towel!

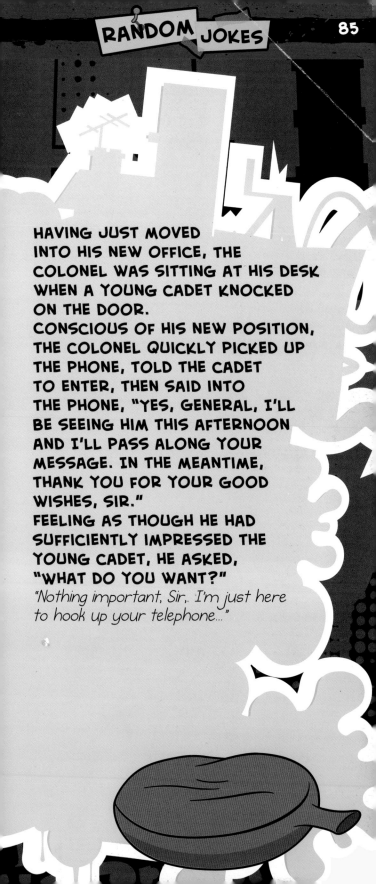

HAVING JUST MOVED
INTO HIS NEW OFFICE, THE
COLONEL WAS SITTING AT HIS DESK
WHEN A YOUNG CADET KNOCKED
ON THE DOOR.
CONSCIOUS OF HIS NEW POSITION,
THE COLONEL QUICKLY PICKED UP
THE PHONE, TOLD THE CADET
TO ENTER, THEN SAID INTO
THE PHONE, "YES, GENERAL, I'LL
BE SEEING HIM THIS AFTERNOON
AND I'LL PASS ALONG YOUR
MESSAGE. IN THE MEANTIME,
THANK YOU FOR YOUR GOOD
WISHES, SIR."
FEELING AS THOUGH HE HAD
SUFFICIENTLY IMPRESSED THE
YOUNG CADET, HE ASKED,
"WHAT DO YOU WANT?"
*"Nothing important, Sir. I'm just here
to hook up your telephone..."*

WHATS GREEN AND GOES ROUND AND ROUND AT 60 MILES PER HOUR?
A frog in a liquidizer!

CURLY: HOW DO YOU SPELL 'EIGHTY'?
Pie-Face: A T!

WHAT DO ELEPHANTS DO IN THE BACK OF A MINI?
They play squash!

WHAT DO YOU CALL SOMEONE WHO STEALS PIGS?
A hamburglar!

Food
JOKES

WHY DID DENNIS'S DAD BLUSH WHEN HE OPENED THE FRIDGE?
He saw the salad dressing!

WHAT DO YOU GET IF YOU CROSS A PUDDING AND A COW PAT?
A smelly jelly!

WHAT'S THE DIFFERENCE BETWEEN BOGEYS AND CABBAGE?
Bea doesn't eat cabbage!

WHAT FLAVOUR OF CRISPS CAN FLY?
Plane crisps!

WHAT IS JAMES BOND'S FAVOURITE CHRISTMAS TREAT?
Mince spices!

WHAT ARE THE STRONGEST VEGETABLES IN THE WORLD?
Muscle sprouts!

WHAT'S YELLOW, GREEN, BROWN AND DANGEROUS?
A three-week old sandwich!

WHAT SITS IN A BOWL OF CUSTARD LOOKING CROSS?
Apple grumble!

WHY SHOULDN'T YOU EAT GREEN ELEPHANTS?
Because they're not ripe yet!

WHAT VEGETABLE SHOULD YOU NEVER HAVE ON A BOAT?
A leek!

MUM: WHY ARE YOU SHIVERING?
Dad: Because you're making me chilli!

WHAT'S A SKELETON'S FAVOURITE BARBECUE DISH?
Spare ribs!

Dennis: Dad, I've just pushed a piece of bacon into the computer CD drive!
DAD: HAS THE COMPUTER STOPPED WORKING?
Dennis: No, but there's a lot of crackling!

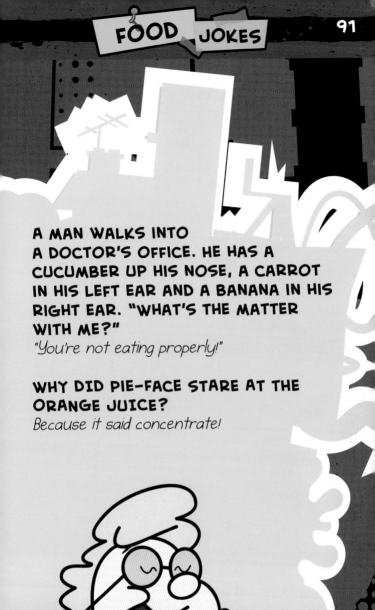

A MAN WALKS INTO
A DOCTOR'S OFFICE. HE HAS A
CUCUMBER UP HIS NOSE, A CARROT
IN HIS LEFT EAR AND A BANANA IN HIS
RIGHT EAR. "WHAT'S THE MATTER
WITH ME?"
"You're not eating properly!"

WHY DID PIE-FACE STARE AT THE
ORANGE JUICE?
Because it said concentrate!

WHAT CHEESE IS MADE BACKWARDS?
Edam!

WHAT FOOD IS BROWN, HAIRY AND FULL OF SNOT?
A coconut with a cold!

WHY DID THE CHEESE PLAY ROULETTE ALL NIGHT?
Because he was on a roll!

WHY DID THE BABY STRAWBERRY CRY?
Because his parents were in a jam!

WHY DID THE BACON GROAN?
Because the egg's yolks were so bad!

MUM: EAT YOUR SPINACH, IT WILL PUT COLOUR IN YOUR CHEEKS.
Dennis: But I don't want green cheeks!

WHAT HAPPENED TO THE MAN WHO STOLE AN APPLE PIE?
He was taken into custard-y!

WHY DID THE GRAPE GO OUT WITH A PRUNE?
Because he couldn't get a date!

**WHY DID THE BAGEL GO
TO THE DENTIST?**
Because it needed a filling!

**WHAT DID THE NUT SAY WHEN
IT SNEEZED?**
Ca-shew!

**WHAT DO YOU GET WHEN
TWO PEAS FIGHT?**
Black-eyed peas!

WHAT DO YOU GET IF YOU PUT THREE DUCKS IN A BOX?
A box of quackers!

HOW DO COMPUTERS EAT?
One byte at a time!

WHAT STARTS WITH A 'T' ENDS WITH A 'T' AND IS FILLED WITH 'T'?
A teapot!

MUM: WHY ARE YOU EATING SO FAST?
Dennis: I don't want to lose my appetite!

WHAT'S GREEN AND WEARS AN APRON?
A cooking apple!

HOW DO YOU MAKE A BANANA SHAKE?
Take it to see a scary movie!

WHAT'S GREEN AND DANGEROUS?
An angry lettuce!

HOW DO YOU KNOW CARROTS ARE GOOD FOR YOUR EYES?
Because you never see a rabbit wearing glasses!

**WHAT'S SMALL,
BROWN AND FLUFFY?**
*A toffee that's been in your
pocket for weeks!*

WHAT'S BROWN, YELLOW AND HAIRY?
Cheese on toast that fell on the carpet!

WHAT'S A PIRATE'S FAVOURITE PUDDING?
Jelly Roger!

WHAT TWO VEGETABLES DO YOU FIND IN THE TOILET?
Leeks and peas!

WHAT KIND OF VEGETABLES DO MATHS TEACHERS EAT?
Square roots!

WHAT SORT OF VEGETABLES DO HISTORY TEACHERS EAT?
Has-beans!

WHAT DO YOU GET IF YOU CROSS A SCOTTISH LEGEND WITH A BAD EGG?
The Loch Ness Pongster!

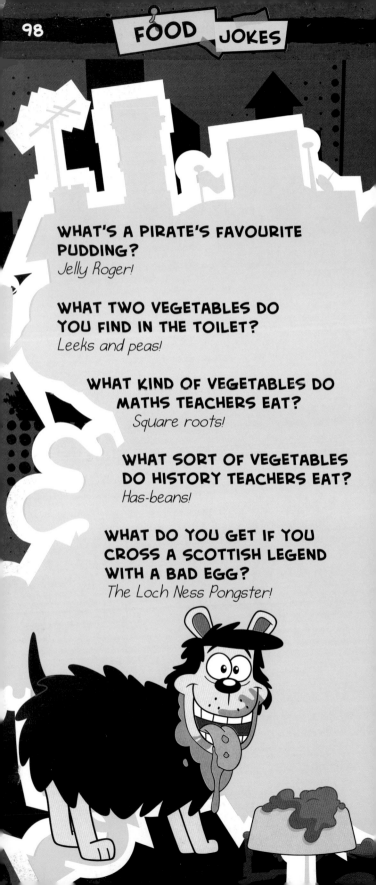

WHAT DID THE ICE CREAM SAY TO THE UNHAPPY CAKE?
'Hey, what's eating you?'

WHY WAS THE BIRTHDAY CAKE AS HARD AS A ROCK?
Because it was a marble cake!

WHY DID THE SILLY BAKER PUT THE BIRTHDAY CAKE IN THE FREEZER?
Because he had been told to ice it!

WHY WAS PIE-FACE STANDING ON HIS HEAD AT THE BIRTHDAY PARTY?
He heard they were having upside-down cake!

HAVE YOU EVER SEEN A MAN-EATING TIGER?
No, but once in a restuurant I saw a man eating chicken!

AN OLD MAN AND A YOUNG MAN WORKED TOGETHER. THE YOUNG MAN HAD NOTICED THAT THE OLDER MAN ALWAYS SEEMED TO HAVE A JAR OF PEANUTS ON HIS DESK. THE YOUNG MAN LOVED PEANUTS.

ONE DAY WHILE THE OLDER MAN WAS AWAY FROM HIS DESK, THE YOUNG MAN COULDN'T RESIST AND WENT TO THE OLD MAN'S JAR AND ATE OVER HALF THE PEANUTS.

WHEN THE OLD MAN RETURNED, THE YOUNG MAN FELT GUILTY AND CONFESSED TO TAKING THE PEANUTS.

The old man responded: "That's ok, since I lost my teeth all I can do is lick the chocolate off my chocolate-coated peanuts!"

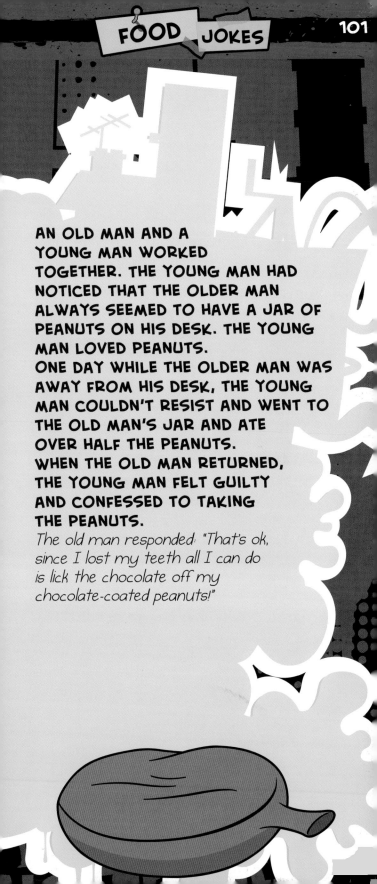

Menu

'WAITER, THIS SOUP TASTES FUNNY.'
'So why aren't you laughing?'

'WAITER, WILL MY PIZZA BE LONG?'
*'No it will be round like
everyone else's!'*

'WAITRESS, DO YOU SERVE CRABS?'
'Certainly, we serve anyone!'

'WAITER, DO YOU HAVE FROGS' LEGS?'
'No, sir. I've always walked like this!'

'HOW DID YOU FIND YOUR DINNER?'
'With a magnifying glass!'

'WAITER, THERE'S A FLY IN MY SOUP!'
*'Don't worry, Sir. The spider in your
salad will eat it.'*

'WAITER, THERE'S A FLY IN MY COFFEE.'
*'Oh don't worry, Sir. He won't
drink much!*

Menu

'WAITER, IS THERE SPAGHETTI ON THE MENU?'
'Yes, I'll just get a cloth and wipe it off!'

'WAITER, THERE'S A FLEA IN MY SOUP"
'Just tell him to hop it!'

'WAITER, THERES A DEAD BEETLE IN MY SOUP'
'Yes, Sir. I'm afraid they're not very good swimmers!'

'WAITER, THERE IS A WASP IN MY PUDDING!'
'So that's where they go in winter!'

'WAITER, THERE IS A SPIDER ON MY PLATE, SEND ME THE MANAGER!'
'That's no good, he's scared of them too!'

WHAT DO YOU GET IF YOU MIX A GYMNAST WITH A BANANA?
A banana split!

WHAT DID THE OGRE SAY TO HER SON WHEN HE WAS EATING HIS DINNER TOO FAST?
Stop goblin your food!

WHAT'S THE MOST POPULAR FOOD GROUP?
The meatles!

WHAT DID DADDY TOMATO SAY TO BABY TOMATO WHEN HE WAS RUNNING BEHIND?
Ketchup!

WHAT ARE THE SPORTIEST KIND OF VEGETABLES?
Runner beans!

WAITER, WHAT IS THIS FLY DOING IN MY SOUP?
Backstroke I believe, Sir!

Silly JOKES

WHAT DO YOU CALL A MAN WHOSE FATHER WAS A CANNON?
A son of a gun!

WHAT DO YOU CALL A DENTIST IN THE ARMY?
A drill sergeant!

WHY DO BICYCLES FALL OVER WHEN THEY ARE LEFT ALONE?
Because they are too tired!

WHAT DO YOU CALL A CHART-TOPPING POP GROUP MADE OF INSECTS?
The lice girls!

**DAD: WHERE'S YOUR
SCHOOL REPORT?**
Dennis: I haven't got it.
DAD: WHY NOT?
*Dennis: Curly borrowed it.
He wanted to scare his parents!*

**WHAT DO YOU SAY TO A
DEAD ROBOT?**
Rust in peace!

IT'S TIME FOR YOUR VIOLIN LESSON.
Oh fiddle!

DAD: THERE'S A MAN AT THE DOOR COLLECTING FOR THE NEW BEANOTOWN SWIMMING POOL.
Dennis: Give him a glass of water!

WHAT HAPPENED WHEN THE WHEEL WAS INVENTED?
It caused a revolution!

DID YOU HEAR ABOUT THE STUPID KAMIKAZE PILOT?
He flew 13 missions!

WHAT DO YOU CALL A TRAFFIC WARDEN WHO NEVER FINES ANYONE?
A terrific warden!

WHAT HAPPENED WHEN THE GIRL DRESSED AS A SPOON LEFT THE HALLOWEEN PARTY?
No one moved. They couldn't stir without her!

WHAT DO YOU CALL A GIRL WITH A FROG IN HER MOUTH?
Lily!

HOW DID THE WITCH DOCTOR ASK THE GIRL TO DANCE?
Voodoo like to dance with me?

WHY DID THE NAUGHTY WIZARD TURN THE GIRL INTO A MOUSE?
Because she ratted on his secret plans!

WHAT DID THE ESKIMO SCHOOL BOY SAY TO THE ESKIMO SCHOOL GIRL?
What's an ice girl like you doing in a place like this?

DO YOU KNOW ALL ABOUT APRIL 1ST?
Yes, I'm fooly aware of it!

WHY IS EVERYONE SO TIRED ON APRIL FOOL'S DAY?
Because they've just finished a long march!

WHAT IS THE BEST TYPE OF BIRTHDAY PRESENT?
Another present!

WHY DID THE BOY PUT CANDLES IN THE TOILET?
He wanted to have a birthday potty!

PIE-FACE: DOCTOR, I GET HEARTBURN EVERY TIME I EAT BIRTHDAY CAKE.
Doctor: Next time, blow out the candles!

WHAT DO YOU CALL A FLY THAT DOESN'T HAVE ANY WINGS?
A walk!

HOW DID THE POLICEMAN CATCH THE BURGLAR WHO HAD CLIMBED UP A TREE?
He used the long arm of the law!

DID YOU HEAR ABOUT THE TREE'S BIRTHDAY?
It was a sappy one!

HOW CAN YOU TELL THAT YOU'RE GETTING OLD?
You go to an antique auction and people start bidding on you!

HOW DO YOU GET THE ASTRONAUT BABY TO SLEEP?
You rock-it!

A BOY WENT TO A HALLOWEEN PARTY WITH A SHEET OVER HIS HEAD. HE WAS ASKED 'ARE YOU A GHOST'?
'No, I'm an unmade bed!'

DID YOU HEAR ABOUT THE DIZZY BOY SCOUT?
He spent all day doing good turns!

WHY DID THE SILLY BOY CARRY A CLOCK AND A BIRD AROUND ON HALLOWEEN?
It was for his 'tick or tweeting'!

DID YOU HEAR ABOUT THE BOY WHO GOT WORRIED WHEN HIS NOSE GREW TO 11 INCHES LONG?
He thought it might turn into a foot!

DID YOU HEAR ABOUT THE BOY WHO WAS KNOWN AS FOG?
He was dense and wet!

HOW DO YOU STOP YOUR LAPTOP BATTERIES RUNNING OUT?
Hide their trainers!

WHY DID THE TAP DANCER LEAVE HIS JOB?
He kept falling in the sink!

WHAT DID ONE TOILET SAY TO THE OTHER?
You look a bit flushed!

WHY DID THE PICTURE GO TO JAIL?
Because it had been framed!

WHAT DO YOU CALL A BOY CALLED LEE WHO NOBODY TALKS TO?
Lone-lee!

WHY DO DRAGONS SLEEP DURING THE DAY?
So they can fight knights!

WHAT DID CINDERELLA SAY WHEN HER PHOTOS DIDN'T SHOW UP?
Some day my prints will come!

WHAT DID THE STAMP SAY TO THE ENVELOPE?
Stick with me and we'll go places!

WHY COULDN'T THE PIRATE PLAY CARDS?
Because he was sitting on the deck!

WHY WAS THE BELT ARRESTED?
For holding up some trousers!

TWO PEANUTS WERE WALKING DOWN THE ROAD...
One of them was a-salted!

HOW DO YOU CATCH A SQUIRREL?
Climb into a tree and act like a nut!

PIE-FACE: WHY ARE THERE SO MANY SMITHS IN THE PHONEBOOK?
Dennis: Because they all have telephones!

WHATS BROWN AND STICKY?
A stick!

THERE ARE THREE TYPES OF PEOPLE IN THE WORLD.
Those who can count, and those who can't!

AS A FARMER IS MILKING HIS COW, A FLY COMES ALONG AND FLIES INTO THE COW'S EAR. A LITTLE BIT LATER, THE FARMER NOTICES THE FLY IN THE MILK AND SAYS:
"Huh. In one ear, out the udder!"

DENNIS: WHAT DO YOU CALL A GULL WHO FLYS OVER THE SEA?
Curly: A seagull.
DENNIS: WHAT DO YOU CALL A GULL THAT FLYS OVER A BAY?
Curly: A bagel?

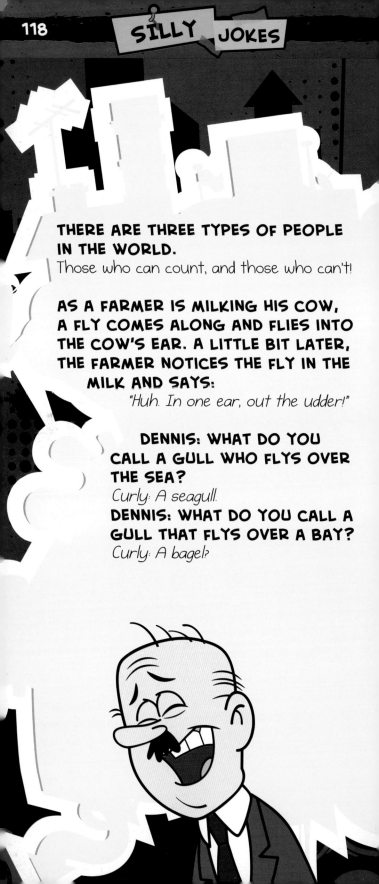

Doctor JOKES

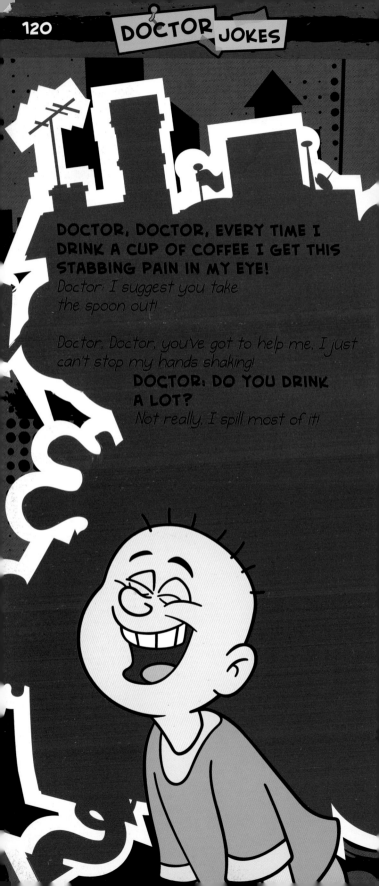

DOCTOR, DOCTOR, EVERY TIME I DRINK A CUP OF COFFEE I GET THIS STABBING PAIN IN MY EYE!
Doctor: I suggest you take the spoon out!

Doctor, Doctor, you've got to help me, I just can't stop my hands shaking!
DOCTOR: DO YOU DRINK A LOT?
Not really, I spill most of it!

DOCTOR, DOCTOR, MY DOG HAS NO NOSE!
Doctor: how does it smell?
TERRIBLE

DOCTOR, DOCTOR, I KEEP THINKING I'M A PENCIL.
Doctor: Can you get to the point?!

DOCTOR, DOCTOR, I THINK I'VE BROKEN MY NECK?
Doctor: Don't worry and keep your chin up!

DOCTOR, DOCTOR, MY BABY IS THE SPITTING IMAGE OF HIS FATHER.
Doctor: Never mind just as long as he's healthy!

Doctor, Doctor, my sister thinks she is a lift!
DOCTOR: WELL TELL HER TO COME IN...
I can't. She doesn't stop at this floor!

DOCTOR, DOCTOR, WHAT CAN I DO? I THINK I'M A PAIR OF CURTAINS?
Doctor: Pull yourself together man!

Doctor, Doctor, I think
I'm a bridge!
DOCTOR: WHAT'S COME OVER YOU?
Oh, two cars, a large truck and a coach!

Doctor, Doctor, I think I'm God
DOCTOR: HOW DID THAT START?
In the beginning there was darkness...!

**DOCTOR, DOCTOR, CAN I HAVE
A SECOND OPINION?**
Doctor: Of course, come
back tomorrow!

DOCTOR JOKES

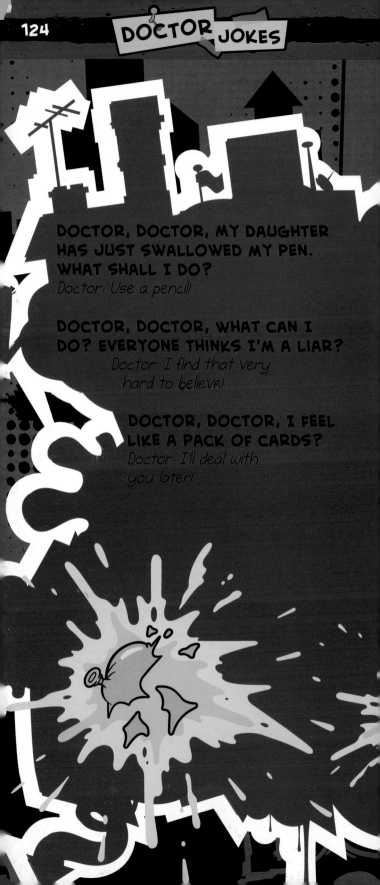

DOCTOR, DOCTOR, MY DAUGHTER HAS JUST SWALLOWED MY PEN. WHAT SHALL I DO?
Doctor: Use a pencil!

DOCTOR, DOCTOR, WHAT CAN I DO? EVERYONE THINKS I'M A LIAR?
Doctor: I find that very hard to believe!

DOCTOR, DOCTOR, I FEEL LIKE A PACK OF CARDS?
Doctor: I'll deal with you later!

DOCTOR, DOCTOR, I'VE JUST SWALLOWED MY MOUTH ORGAN.
Doctor: Well look on the bright side, at least you weren't playing a grand piano!

Doctor, Doctor, I think I'm a cat!
DOCTOR: HOW LONG HAS THIS BEEN GOING ON?
Oh, since I was a kitten I guess!

**DOCTOR, DOCTOR,
I'VE GOT INSOMNIA**
Doctor: Just sit on the edge
of the bed. You'll soon drop off!

**DOCTOR, DOCTOR, MY
HAIR IS FALLING OUT.
CAN YOU GIVE ME
SOMETHING TO KEEP
IT IN?**
Doctor: Certainly, here's a box!

**DOCTOR, DOCTOR,
I THINK I'M SHRINKING.**
Doctor: Well, you'll just have
to be a little patient!

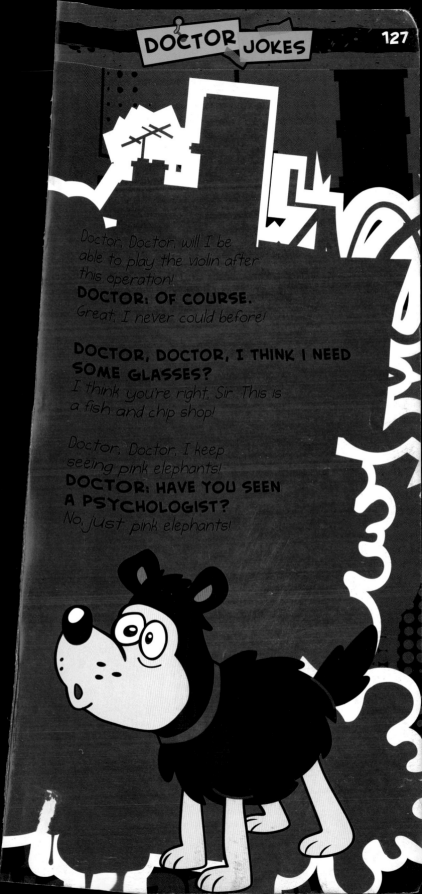

Doctor, Doctor, will I be able to play the violin after this operation!

DOCTOR: OF COURSE.

Great, I never could before!

DOCTOR, DOCTOR, I THINK I NEED SOME GLASSES?

I think you're right, Sir This is a fish and chip shop!

Doctor, Doctor, I keep seeing pink elephants!

DOCTOR: HAVE YOU SEEN A PSYCHOLOGIST?

No, just pink elephants!

10 THINGS YOU DON'T WANT TO HEAR A DOCTOR SAY!

'Oops, has anyone seen my watch?'

'Darn, page 47 of the manual is missing!'

'Come back with that, bad dog!'

'If this is his spleen, what was that we just removed?'

'Can you stop that heart from beating, it's putting me off.'

'I'm legally blind without my glasses. Oops, that's broken it!'

'Everybody stop, I've lost one of my contact lenses!'

'Hand me that... uh... thingy over there!'

'Darn, there go the lights again!'

'Did you need both those lungs?'